GHOST STORIES
OF
LANCASTER COUNTY
PENNSYLVANIA

By

Dorothy Burtz Fiedel

Copyright © 1995 Dorothy Burtz Fiedel

Printed in the United States of America
Science Press
300 W. Chestnut St.
Ephrata, Pa 17522
Published by Dorothy Burtz Fiedel
All Photos by Dorothy Burtz Fiedel unless otherwise indicated

All rights reserved. No part of this book may be used or reproduced without express written consent of the author and publisher, except in the case of brief quotations embodied in critical essays and reviews.

ISBN 0-9640254-1-8

Cover Photo—Cemetery located along Route 999, Manor Township, Lancaster County, Pa. Photo by D. B. Fiedel.

To My Husband
Sam
*. . . who makes me feel good in living life,
a place we've been forever.*

Table of Contents

Science and Shadows	1
A Visitor From Another Century	6
Last Room On The Left	9
An Unfair Trade	13
Manor Street Mystery	16
Beast In The Basement	18
Three Mile Isle of Misfortune	23
The Enchanted Garden At The Rail Road House	29
Top Hat And Tails	33
Uncommon Knowledge	37
Pennsylvania Pow Wow Doctors	41
Who Are You Going To Call?	47
Hempfield Haunting	54
Odds And Ends, Bits And Pieces	57
So You Want to See A Ghost?	60
Marietta Ghost Walk	61
Acknowledgements	64
Footnotes	65

Science and Shadows

"Good Lord, deliver us," echoed the congregation. They were responding during a prayer delivered by their clergy who asked God's protection:

> "... From ghosties and ghoulies
> and long-leggidy beasties
> And things that go bump
> In the night..." *Cornish Liturgy*[1]

For centuries, the belief in the super-natural has peppered the lives, beliefs, customs and religions of man throughout recorded and unrecorded history. We find links between Ageless Wisdom and our Founding Fathers which are never reported in traditional history books. For instance, there is a story of an unknown man who gave an inspiring speech to the delegates at the Continental Congress as they hesitiated to sign the Declaration of Independence, saying, "God has given America to be free... Sign, and not only for yourselves, for that parchment will be the textbook of freedom, the bible of the rights of man forever!"[2]

None present knew him, or at least didn't admit to knowing him, but somehow he managed to enter and leave a locked and guarded room unnoticed.[3] Some say he was the mysterious one known as "the Professor." A vegetarian, who drank no liquor, and spent most of his time studying rare books and ancient manuscripts; he appeared to be on close personal terms with Washington, Franklin, and Paine. A young man of over 70 years in 1776, he spoke about the previous century as if he had lived it.[4]

It is strange how George Washington believed he was guided by higher sources which helped him predict British troop movements with amazing accuracy. Anthony Sherman, who was with Washington at Valley Forge, reported an incident which happened there in which Washington had a vision of an Angelic presence. Washington was shown the birth, progress, and destiny of the United States. He was told that: "while the stars remain and the heavens send down dew upon the earth, so long shall the Republic last. The whole world united shall never be able to prevail against her. Let every child of the Republic learn to live for his God, his land, and the Union."[5]

Many who read this bit of information may think the cold at Valley Forge froze more than just toes and somehow caused old George to become delusional. However, one must remember that Washington, who refused a salary for leading our fledging nation, was the inventor of the expense account. Washington's bill for eight years of service included 6 percent per annum interest on his out of pocket expenses, plus a surcharge for depreciation. His expenses totaled close to half-a-million dollars, an enormous sum when one takes into consideration that full General's pay for that eight years would have amounted to about $48,000. Exhibiting a shrewd business head, with obviously no brain damage, his expense account seems to have served as the revered model of our current-day federal budget.[6]

Where will I be after I die? is a question all must ask themselves at least once in a life-time.

"I will be nowhere," has been an unacceptable answer from before recorded time. Ever since the first burial of the dead some 50,000 years ago, burials have been ritual occasions celebrating a transition in continued time and not a final ending.[7] The Neanderthal man placed flowers with its dead; others placed food, ornaments, and weapons. Powerful people were often buried with their servants, murdered for the occasion, so that they were ready to serve their master or mistress in another world that continued in time.[8]

What then is the barrier that separates the quick and the dead? The barrier is not death but time.

The nature of time was discussed by the ancient Greek philosophers Plato and Aristotle. The beginning of the scientific revolution of the sixteenth century found cosmological scientists such as Isaac Newton, dealing with the question of time. Subject matter that was once traditionally a philosophical activity.[9]

The twentieth century dawned as the great age of discovery in physics. Albert Einstein's general and special theories of relativity, forever linked space and time. His theories laid the ground work for today's quantum mechanics, string theories (which suggest there must be either ten or twenty-six dimensions, most of them hidden from our awareness)[10], tachyons (theorized high speed particles beyond the light barrier where time flows backward)[11], black holes (theorized singularities so dense even light cannot escape), cosmic wormholes (mathematical theorized tunnels through space-time serving as a gateway to the past)[12], and more interesting theories much too involved to discuss at length in this brief over-view.

In 1920 Einstein denied firmly that time travel might be theoretically possible. Two decades later, in reviewing a paper on relativity, he admitted that on a cosmic scale it is merely "a matter of convention to say that A precedes B rather than vice versa.[13]

In other words, to put it on a more human scale, consider this. *Did 97 year old Ethel Mackrackin meet her death: (A) before, or (B) after her bungi cord broke?*

It may also just be a matter of convention to say it is impossible to pass between the barrier of time dividing life and death, for many have witnessed or experienced events that suggest it happens.

For instance, in Mark Nesbitt's *Ghosts of Gettysburg,* the author tells of two former Gettysburg College administrators who took an elevator trip into another century. Expecting to stop on the first floor, their "vertical wormhole" continued down to basement level and the door opened to reveal, ". . . not the area once cleaned up for storage, but a scene out of time and reason, the blood stained doctors and orderlies of a century before, again performing their abhorrent and hideous tasks of slicing sinew and sawing bone. . . ."[14]

The stories you are about read are true. Answers or explanations for how or why they occurred may never be found. This mystery may explain the universal interest stories such as these hold for young and old, in all walks of life, world-wide.

Since publishing my first book, *Haunted Lancaster County Pennsylvania: Ghosts and Other Strange Occurrences*, I've had the opportunity to speak to many people about the supernatural. Much to my surprise, a few said they didn't read books such as these, for they feared being frightened or scared by things they didn't or couldn't understand.

To them I urge that they employ a healthy and robust sense of humor to all of life's mysteries. Sometimes it is one's own fear and coincidental circumstances that can transform an everyday situation into an "other-worldly" experience. For example, there are at least four people who had a Lancaster County "tour-of-their-life" a few years back.

About twenty years ago I was one of the small nucleus of paid, full-time tour guides at Wheatland, the Lancaster, Pa. presidential home of James Buchanan, fifteenth president of the United States. It was also home to his niece, Harriet Lane who served as "first lady" for her bachelor uncle.

It was one of those hot summer days which come in late September, about 4:30 in the afternoon, just before closing time. A sudden thunderstorm was brewing and I was given the "ok" to call it a day.

I rushed to the third floor former servant's quarters to don street clothes, hoping to beat the violent weather crashing outside. I swallowed hard as I ascended the dark stairway leading to the changing room. Working quickly, just as I was about to step out of my hoop skirt, I heard a voice loudly whisper, "Dorothy... Dorothy!" The room suddenly lit up with a flash of lightening, almost simultaneously vibrating with a roll of thunder, "Boy!...", I thought, "... I sure hope that isn't Harriet Lane!"

Of course, it wasn't. It was one of my co-workers telling me of last minute visitors and asking if I would pick them up on the second floor to finish their tour. Consenting, I hurried to get back into my Victorian costume and scurried down the steps pausing at the doorway which opened onto the second floor. My intent was to silently slip into position at the large, gift-of-state procelain bowl which sat at the top of the stairs, a spot located no more than three paces from where I stood. I made my move. The door groaned as my entrance was perfectly timed with blinding light and a thunder clap so loud that it tickled the pit of one's stomach.

Now, I was having a bad hair day . . . but that certainly didn't explain the blood curdling screams that echoed through Wheatland at that moment. I froze as I came face to face with two men and one woman, faces contorted with screams, as a second screaming woman, arms flailing in the air, headed downstairs. The one on the run, at the first curve, suddenly remembered her abandoned friends, stopped, white-knuckled on the rail.

I gushed apologies; it was not my intent to frighten them but the storm rumbled on causing me to intermittently pause in lieu of shouting over the thunder claps. As any experienced guide knows, it is imperative to seize immediate intellectual control of any size group, within the first thirty seconds of greeting. I definitely had their undivided attention, but I don't think they heard a word I said.

I was about five minutes into the tour, standing at the entrance to Buchanan's bedroom as my guests, still as white as salt pillars, and one dabbing at beads of perspiration, started darting furtive glances between the portrait above the bedroom fireplace and myself. The portrait was of Buchanan's fiancee, Ann Coleman, who some say committed suicide after a lover's spat; the devastated Buchanan never married. Over the years, many guests, including my boss, Mrs. Clair Parker, remarked about a resemblance between Ann Coleman and myself. I didn't see it, . . . but boy, I sure knew that was the wrong time to be "recognized".

At that particular moment, I might as well have been giving a tour of the Bates Motel. Ashened faced, one of the men turned and blurted out, "Are you related to the lady in the portrait?"

"No . . .", my reply was accented by a crash and a flash, ". . . some say I resemble her."

The rest of the tour was uneventful except that any step I took toward my guests caused them to back up five. At the back bedroom, the one where Buchanan died, I motioned to the stairs and bid my guests farewell. Timidly, one woman asked me to hold out my arm. Puzzled, I did. I was firmly pinched by four people as they scurried down the stairs and out of the Twilight Zone.

A Visitor From Another Century

The house on Union Street in Columbia has stood since the late 1800's, but maybe its nineteenth century owner still walks the floors unaware that death had separated him from his beloved home.

Elizabethtown resident, Rick Able, wrote to tell me a story which he had heard many times over the years. It was his father and grandmother who witnessed the event. His grandmother freely spoke of the incident over the years; his father confirmed it, however, with much reluctance.

It happened one evening in the late 1930's in the Able's home on Union Street in Columbia. Rick's father was a boy of 8 or 9 years old at the time and was lying on the bed with his mother in a bedroom at the top of the stairs on the second floor.

They were listening to the radio and talking when suddenly they heard footsteps softly, slowly, coming up the stairs. Both expected to see Father come through the door; the conversation stopped.

Finally, in the doorway appeared not Father, but a man dressed in nineteenth century clothing and wearing a top hat. The gentleman stood motionless in the entry way and then in a few seconds faded out of sight.

"Did you see that?" the boy's mother said. "Yes!" was the stunned boy's reply.

Rick Able, in describing his grandmother wrote: ". . . (she) was born in 1908 in Washington Boro, (and) always spoke of the spirited, *The Seventh Book of Moses,* having a true sixth sense, and attributing this to the fact she was born with 'a veil over her head': at that time it was believed that this would endow one born with such (a veil) to have an insight into the spirit world, and more generally great sensitivity and precognitive abilities that just cannot be explained."

The Sixth Book of Moses and *The Seventh Book of Moses,* to which Mr. Able refers, were and are indeed considered magical texts.

Also known as "Moses' Magical Spirit-Art", known as the Wonderful Arts of the old, wise Hebrews, its text is taken from the Mosaic Books of the Cabala and Talmud, for the good of Mankind.[1]

Their texts date back to times before the Christian Era. Ammon Monroe Aurand, Jr., author of *The "Pow Wow" Book,* explains that: "... the *Sixth and Seventh Books of Moses* is the common term for the magical works of the Jewish law-giver ... Moses apparently acquired his knowledge of magical practices from the Egyptians, as it is recorded in the Old Testament that he was learned in all the wisdom of the Egyptians and mighty in words and in deeds."[2]

Aurand also writes concerning the texts:

> "INSTRUCTION. These two books were revealed by God, the Almighty, to his faithful servant Moses, on Mount Sinai, *intervale lucis,* and in this manner they also came into the hands of Aaron, Caleb, Joshua, and finally to David and his son Solomon and their high priest Sadlock. Therefore, they are *Bibliis arcanum arcanorum,* which means, Mystery of all Mysteries."[3]

The mysterious man in the top hat had appeared to Mrs. Able once again, decades later. Lying downstairs on a couch she was awakened by the confused whimper, a half-bark of the family dog, a black Labrador Retriever.

There in front of her stood the same man dressed in nineteenth century clothing with a top hat on his head. The man disappeared as before in just a few seconds, leaving a very frightened and confused hunting dog.

"My grandmother never feared the apparition. She often told me not to be afraid. 'Just make the sign of the cross and ask it, what do you want of me?' " explained her grandson.

Rick's father was more pragmatic. He never spoke of anything eerie or unusual, almost scoffing at the prospect. When questioned thru the years, even as a man in his 60's, his only response would be, "Yeah, I saw it . . . and I don't want to talk about it."

Rick Able clearly explained, "He didn't care to discuss what he couldn't explain."

Last Room on the Left

Today, a newborn's first glimpse of the world could be the sterile surroundings of a hospital delivery room. Many times, the last glimpse of the world is also a hospital room. No other institution in our society is the site of so many entrances and exits of the human spirit. But do all the spirits make their exit or is it possible they just hang around in a certain wing, on a certain floor, down a certain hall, in the last room on the left?

Some of the earliest hospital care dates to the thirteenth century. The first hospitals, which were numerous all over Europe, were of white-washed wood. Later, they were two- and three-story marble-pillared buildings around open courtyards, elaborately decorated like the palaces of the day. The first were founded by monasteries, but with the rise of the middle-class and secular rule, kings and queens and bankers founded and endowed them and city administrations ran them. The early hospitals were built outside the city walls to separate infectious patients from the rest of the population.[1]

The towns, however, were incubators of disease. Overcrowding, polluted wells, primitive sanitation, streets swarming with pigs and rats-these bred typhus, typhoid and influenza. The worst disease of all was the bubonic plague, or the Black Death. It struck in the 1340's cutting a swath of death across Europe. Estimates of the death toll range from one fourth to one half of Europe's entire population.[2]

The Lancaster County cholera epidemic in September 1854 certainly didn't kill as many people as the plague did in Europe. It raged through the town of Columbia leaving many dead in its wake. Within 16 days, 126 people were dead.[3]

Lancaster City, however, had cholera deaths one month prior to Columbia's epidemic losing 28 people to the pestilence in August of that year.[4]

In 1854 not all cities or communities had a facility for caring for the sick. This was the case in Columbia. Lancaster had the Lancaster County Hospital (established 1830). The Lancaster Alms House also cared for members of the community, however, these patients were medically considered insane or too feeble to care for themselves.[5]

Today, hospitals are so numerous that most communities have a choice of professional care. For specialized care, one might choose a different doctor, or a different hospital.

Choosing a room in a hospital is a different story. When a patient checks in, he is given a room description.

"Private or semi-private?" says the desk clerk in the Admitting Office.

Perhaps a better question might be: "Haunted, not haunted, haunted only part of the time, haunted only on a full moon or during a lunar eclipse..."

One particular hospital, which shall remain nameless, has a room which is never occupied for very long.

"It's right down there," she said as she pointed, then quickly glanced around thinking someone might guess what she was revealing to me. "Not long ago, we had another patient insist on being moved in the middle of the night," she said.

Another employee verified the story with a wide-eyed nod saying, "We have a problem with that room; patients complain about it. One patient said he didn't care if he was rolled into the hall for the night... just get him out!"

The story unfolded as five different people told much the same tale. What is interesting, is that none of the patients who experienced the ghostly inhabitants were sedated or under the influence of medication, a matter-of-fact which would understandably be the first consideration of a medical staff.

"Patients who occupy that room are only in for one or two days, usually after a short procedure not requiring pain medication or sedation, just observation for a short stay," explained one witness.

According to the witnesses, the room has more than one

ghost. The last patient who requested removal described pretty much what all patients describe. The room is occupied by the spirits of four men. Each is a different nationality, one Caucasian, one Negro, one of Spanish descent, and one Oriental ... sounds a little like the United Nations.

These four fellows make a general nuisance of themselves. They mill around the room talking among themselves. Sometimes they talk to the startled patients, making it almost impossible to get a good night's sleep.

"The last fellow we moved said he thought he was hallucinating. The ghosts in the room got noisier and noisier, and the more he tossed and turned, the louder they talked. The last straw came when he opened his eyes and one was sitting on the end of his bed. The patient turned his head, catching a glimpse of something out of the corner of his eye, and one of the other ghosts was sitting on his night-stand, more solid in appearance, but not quite solid enough ... then the patient noticed the telephone sitting behing the man. I guess you could say he saw right through him ... that's when he pushed his 'call' button and started yelling for someone to get him out of there," explained one of the hospital workers.

She continued, "That patient was really upset. We don't exactly know what to tell them, but what they've experienced is very much the same as other patients. They haven't hallucinated ... even some of the staff don't like to go into that room—especially the Night Shift."

The cycle of life and death and life goes on in every hospital in the world. Why are four spirits spending so much time in that last room on the left? Are they the unwilling victims of tragic accidents, did they waste away from disease or did they die by their own hand? Maybe one was a doctor so devoted he refuses to leave a place that is his last link with the living. Are the ghostly-four lonely or a do they have a sense of humor? Do they have, at least, a sense of compassion and do not haunt rooms where patients are gravely ill?

Hopefully, this story will not cause anyone who is faced with a hospital stay to hestiate because they fear meeting a hospital ghost. Remember, the forms that glide hospital hallways at night, slipping silently into and out of the rooms are usually the dedicated nurses and resident doctors who so tirelessly and compassionately minister to the needs of the sick.

That frightening shiver that shoots up the spine, the shock that opens all clogged sinuses, and the deer-in-the-headlight stare that signals sheer terror, you won't experience in the hospital; that comes when you ... open the bill ... open the bill ... open the bill ...

An Unfair Trade

My husband and I spend a lot of time waiting in the supermarket check-out line. It is there we found out that Soviet engineers found hell while drilling for oil in Siberia. Of course, other issues of the same tabloid magazine featured a photo of First Lady Hillary Clinton and her newly adopted space-alien baby, and a feature story about a woman who exploded after eating 200 pounds of potatoes.

All of these stories sound incredible. Probably all of them are . . . except maybe hell and its exact location.

Hell is a concept that has been around for centuries. One might call it the "cosmic disposal site for the wicked."[1]

In ancient Greece, the damned simply spent eternity lying face down in a swamp of mud and frogs.[2]

During the 1700's, scientists theorized that hell was on the sun or aboard a comet.[3]

Alan Berstein, a University of Arizona history professor, says the Jewish concept of hell grew out of frustration with injustice.[4]

During the second century B.C., it was obvious that people were getting away with sin in this life so the Jews began looking for punishment in the next. They found it; its name is Gehenna, named for a garbage dump near Jerusalem where waste and animal carcasses were cast into fires.[5]

Christianity also has its hell. Many a preacher has expounded on the "fire and brimstone" idea of hell. The Bible describes it as a "lake of fire," "weeping and gnashing of teeth," "outer darkness," and a "worm that never dies."[6]

Pick up the newspaper today and it is obvious that people are still getting away with sin in this life, just as they were in the second century B.C. Maybe crimes against man and society would decrease if more people knew that in the end the devil will come to collect his due.

This is just what happened to a man who called me in 1993. He was very sincere when he said, "I now tell all my friends that they better be careful what they wish for . . . they just might get it."

James, as I shall call him, couldn't remember exactly when he started to stray off the path. His mother has always taught him the "right" things in life. He was taught about God, and the importance of love and respect for his fellow man. He strayed and found himself associating with a pretty "rough" crowd of people.

He first caught glimpses of this "dark entity" in his home. He described it as a "dark shadow" that would dart across the hall, or through the living room. Many times it was something he would "sense" rather than visually see. He also noticed that during the period of time he and his wife were doing an unusual amount of arguing, the frequency of the "dark shadow's" visits would increase.

After one particularly nasty fight, his wife stormed upstairs. A few minutes later she came flying down, obviously hysterical. He explained: "After going into the bedroom, she suddenly had that strange feeling she was not alone. Then she heard it . . . it sounded like a growling dog, snapping and snarling his chops at her. There was nothing there in front of her but the vicious snarls without a source. She ran downstairs screaming . . . she was hysterical."

His most enlightening experience was yet to come. It happened after a violent traffic accident as he lay hovering between life and death.

James explained: "I lay close to death for sometime. The doctors didn't expect me to live. If I did survive, which was doubtful, I wasn't expected to ever walk again. My legs were badly injured. Time seemed to stand still. Ten minutes in the hospital passed like ten hours . . . of course, I was heavily sedated, but even through the sedation, I knew 'what' came to visit me. It was a dark shadow that hovered near my bed. It didn't look 'like' anything, but I knew it was the devil. He was there for one reason. . . ."

James explained how the entity offered him a "deal." The "darkness" told James he would make a trade: he would let James walk, but James had to give him his soul in exchange.

James spoke of that fateful moment: "I was not afraid of it. I refused to look at it; I kept my face turned away. Then I told it . . . 'in Jesus's name, leave me alone.' No deal! I wanted no part of it."

James survived. He does walk, but with crutches and with pain and difficulty. Each step for him is an accomplishment, a personal triumph over gravity, over pain and suffering and over evil.

Although the path ahead of him is a physically difficult one to walk, it is straight, narrow and softly illuminated; for he has seen the darkness and chosen the light.

When his journey through life is over, when the last trumpet blows, he'll stand before his maker—a whole man—body and soul.

Manor Street Mystery

It seems as if Manor Street in Columbia has more than its fair share of haunted houses. In fact, this house and the house referred to in "Beast In The Basement" (see page 18) are either situated next door to each other or are one in the same.

Exact locations can be deceiving. Sometimes a dwelling, 50 years ago, might have been used as a single family home. As the years pass, and properties change hands, these buildings are often converted into apartment houses sometimes causing street numbers to change. However, I will not reveal exact locations for either residence.

David Germeyer, of Columbia, wrote to tell me about a very strange experience he had many years ago.

The year was 1963. David was in the sixth grade.

He was playing at a friend's house who's family lived in an apartment on Manor Street. Enjoying themselves with baseball cards and the usual "guy" talk, all of a sudden they were startled to hear a scuffle in the hallway outside the living room door.

Much to their surprise they heard a woman yelling, "You're hurting me!" They listened as she loudly gasped for breath. Dull, heavy thuds shook the air as she was pounded against the hallway wall.

Frightened and not knowing exactly what to do, David suggested they crack the living room door and look out. Agreeing, their hearts pounded as David slowly opened the entry into the hall.

David recalls, "There was complete silence, nothing was in the hallway. We stood there with the door totally open now and we both looked at each other. We were puzzled. I remember saying to my friend, 'We heard that, right?' and he acknowledged it."

It was something David said he would have forgotten about, except it happened again, several weeks later. It was the same scenario, except this time, they both agreed to swing the door wide open.

Hoping to see the pair who were repeating the violent fight, they were astounded to find ... nothing. The hallway was completely empty. No trace of the two people who so loudly made their presence known could be found.

"I'm forty years old now, and every time I drive past that house I get the willies," says David.

David should be happy to hear that he has company in the Manor Street "willies" department.

Beast in the Basement

Memories of a childhood home can be both sweet and sour. The scent of freshly baked bread, or the taste of a cold glass of lemonade can trigger pleasant memories. The sight of an old homestead, for many, brings back the recollections of a simpler time.

Martin, a Columbia businessman, feels something quite different when he passes his old home. A ball forms in the pit of his stomach and then he remembers the beast in the basement.

"It still gives me the creeps," he said, ". . . even though its been so many years ago."

Martin was one of eleven children who lived in a home on Manor Street in Columbia (the exact location I will not reveal). Martin's mother lived at that address all her life; Martin lived there about twenty years. According to him, he and his brothers and sisters had a good, healthy fear of the house, especially of the cellar.

"You had to be mighty brave to go down there! Even if I drive by the house today, a grown man, it still gives me the willies," he said, stoned faced.

Martin and his brothers and sisters refused to enter the house if their mother and father were not home. An empty house was a rare occurrence; but sometimes their mother might run a necessary errand while their father was at work. The children, finding no strength in numbers, would patiently wait outside until their courage arrived.

What was it that so frightened that Columbia family? Before I tell of Martin's experiences, lets first look at the history of the area.

The whole of Lancaster County, for hundreds, even thou-

Looking East on Manor Street in Columbia, Pa.

sands of years, was occupied by successive Indian tribes. The book, *An Authentic History of Lancaster County*, written in 1869, says it was common at that period of time to find arrowheads, tomahawks, hatchets, stone-pipes and pieces of pottery turned up with the plow.[1] Today, in 1995, Indian artifacts can still be found in the freshly tilled soil.

The town of Columbia stands on an old Shawanah Indian town. When John Wright came through the area in 1724 there were Shawanese Indians quartered in about two or three dozen tepees and log huts along the Shawanese (Shawnee) Run and an adjacent run.[2]

Archaeological discoveries as early as 1816 point at much older inhabitants. The following is an extract from a letter written by Joel Lightner, Esq., Salisbury, Lancaster County, Pa. to the Reverend Mr. Shaffer, New York, dated November 30, 1816:

"... a large bone was found ... the length (of which) ... is fifteen inches, and measures ten and a half inches around the smaller solid part; the circumference of the thicker or upper part is twenty-two inches, but the thickest part could not be preserved ... This bone was found lying partly in a horizontal position ... and appeared to have been thrown there promiscuously, as well as the pieces of limestone around it, which are evidently fragments of larger ones, ... Since the discovery of these bones on my land, I have been informed that many years since, an extraordinary large tooth (grinder) was found in a spring about two miles from my quarry, but I am not able to learn what has become of it."[3]

Indian artifacts found in the area over the years have striking similarities to other parts of the world. Enamel beads found in Indian graves in Lancaster County are very similar to ones found in burial sites in Beverly, Canada, Stockholm, Sweden and another from a grave in Jutland (a division of Denmark, formerly comprising the whole continental portion of the Danish dominion).

A. Morlot (of Lausanne, Switzerland) in 1862 concluded that; "... America appears to have been visited already at that remote period by Europeans, most likely by those skillful navigators, the Phoenicians."[4]

Picture-writing on rocks located below Safe Harbor are other indications linking early civilizations of Lancaster County with the ancient Phoenicians. These rocks are only visible when the Susquehanna River water level is very low.

A written account about these figures was written in 1865 by Professor T. C. Porter, D.D., formerly of Lancaster. He writes:

"The two rocks contain in all upwards of 80 distinct figures, and a number more almost obliterated. They are much scattered, and seem to have been formed without regard to order, so that it is not possible for an unskilled observer to say that they bear any necessary relation to each other. They are probably symbolical, but it is left to those who are versed in American antiquities to decipher their meaning. Some points, however, are clear. They are made by the Aborigines, and made at a large cost of time and labor, with rude stone implements, because no sharp lines or cuts betray the uses of iron or steel. This, in connection with their number and variety, proves that they were not the offspring of idle fancy or the work of idle hours, but the product of design toward some end of high importance in the eyes of the sculptors."[5]

What has all this got to do with that house on Manor Street, Columbia? Martin's house seemed to be inhabited by some unknown entity whose domain stretched from cellar to attic, and just possibly over time.

It was next to impossible to keep a good light bulb in the attic light fixtures. "It would burn out . . . all the time, . . . dozens and dozens of times," said Martin.

Not only that, it sounded to the family as if someone was upstairs, kicking the attic door. While tucked in at night, the racket was terrible. There was the sound of chains that seemed to rattle, down the stairways.

He told of a particularly noisy night when a loud thumping echoed throughout the place, quite like the sound made if someone threw a chair down the steps. His father, who was sleeping in bed at the time, sat bolt upright in bed, the color drained from his face.

The racket was so bad at times that neighbors were called to help search through the home. One night they even called Columbia Boro police who conducted a thorough sweep of the place which turned up absolutely nothing.

Martin's mother had a name for the strange occurrences. She called them "tokens," or signs of something to come. These "tokens" came in the form of pictures flying off the walls, or china breaking, but the most curious of them all occurred in the cellar-many times.

The walls of the cellar were made of stone and on a yearly basis, these stone walls were white-washed with a lime and water mixture. Of course, the fresh coat of white-wash helped to visually brighten and tidy the room, but the white-washing was also done to cover the "beast." The beast was in the form of a charcole-like line drawing of a bear. It appeared on one wall of the cellar. No matter how thick the coat of white-wash, nor how often it was applied, a few days later this bear figure would burn through to take its place on the cellar wall.

It was scrubbed, and rubbed, then painted. Still, the distinct outline of a bear would reappear.

A bear on the stone wall of the inner most recesses of a home is curious. However, in another time, another age, pictures of wild animals were drawn on the stone walls of man's home.

This kind of artwork is the earliest known to modern man. It occurred during the Paleolithic stage of human development about 35,000 years ago.

At that time the last Ice Age was coming to an end and the humans of that period liked to live in caves or under rock over-hangs. Some of the most striking works of art are images of animals, incised, painted, or sculptured, on the rock surfaces of caves. Many of which have been found in the caverns of Altamira in northern Spain, or in the caverns at Lascaux, France.[6]

Bison, deer, horses and cattle race across walls and ceilings of these caves in wild profusion, some of them simply outlined in black, others filled in with bright earth colors.[7]

The pictures never occur near the mouth of a cave, where they would be open to easy view (and destruction) but only in the darkest recesses.[8]

Scientists say that there can be little doubt that they were produced as part of a magic ritual, perhaps to ensure a successful hunt.

"Draw the animal and they will come," thought the caveman artist.

Lines thought to represent darts or spears are sometimes found pointing at the animals. There is also a peculiar disorder in the way the images are superimposed on one another. Apparently, people of the Old Stone Age made no clear distinction between image and reality; by making a picture of an animal they meant to bring the animal itself within their grasp, and in "killing" the image they thought they had killed the animal's vital spirit. So a "dead" image lost its potency after the killing ritual had been performed, and could be disregarded when the spell had to be renewed.[9]

This kind of "emotional attachment" may seem primitive, but it is not unlike the way modern man thinks. Many people carry images of loved ones in their wallet. People have also been known to tear up the photo of someone they have come to hate.[10]

Was Martin's childhood home located on the site where a far older family lived? Did the rocks used to build the old home's foundation once serve as the shelter of an ancient hunter? If so, did the hunter ever bag his bear?

The Three Mile Isle of Misfortune

She lays long and lush in the Susquehanna River, a channel separating her from the shore of Dauphin County, her southern most tip jutting into Lancaster County. Who would think that such a serene setting could be the sight of the worst nuclear accident in United States history?

Just why Three Mile Island's Unit 2 reactor chose March 28, 1979 to belch radio-active steam into the atmosphere is a mystery. But history and local old-timers indicate that March has meant trouble at least three other times in the present century.[1] The now infamous site has brought misfortune to anyone in possession of it dating back to the days of William Penn.[2]

My first memories of the island drift back to my childhood, or to the island's pre-reactor days. My friend and I rowed the river in a water-logged wooden boat. It was a two-man craft; one rowed; one bailed. Our excursions took us to either Shelly Island (a good two mile round-trip row), or down the wide channel to Three Mile Island.

We were prepared for anything, or so we thought. Our provisions consisted of a few packs of crackers, a bag of potato chips, a cooler of ice water, and two Maxwell House coffee cans (one was our spare bailer).

It was always "safety-first" with us. Our life-saving equipment consisted of a floatation pillow, more accurately described as a "rock with straps."

The island channel trips always stand out in my memory as being rather spooky. Several times we found ourselves bobbing in the thick, green, river channel about mid-island, quite close to dusk. This area, just about where the cooling tower over Reactor Number 2 is now located, was once a cornfield. It was here we watched for deer and hoped we might catch a glimpse of buckskin and feathers, thinking maybe at least one Indian was still alive and well and living on the island. That spot in the river always set our hair on end and with renewed energy, we rowed and bailed for our very lives. Little did we know that place would be the source of trouble and fear, magnified a thousand-fold, a few years down the line.

There is one person alive today who knows better than anyone that "trouble" is the island's middle-name. Her name is Elaine Huber, a researcher and historian who has spent the last 8 years digging into the past of that little chunk of Susquehanna River real estate. It is only through her kindness and generosity in providing me with copies of several of her published articles on the subject, that I am able to enlighten the reader about the island's checkered past. The following account is drawn solely from her research.

Young Thomas Cookson left his native England and arrived in the wild and woolly place in Penn's province called Lancaster. The young lawyer settled in quite nicely performing his duties recording deeds, keeping the peace, and governing as chief burgess.[3]

An ambitious fellow, he took on the responsibility of serving as Penn's Deputy Surveyor of Lancaster County, a job which took him out into the far reaches of the county which was then three or four times larger than it is today. That is when the nice, big island along the eastern shore of the treacherous Conewago Falls caught his eye.[4]

He wanted to add the piece of property to the 2,000 acres of shoreline next to the island he already owned. So in a December 1749 business letter to Thomas Penn, he tacked on a request to "purchase this Island on ye Common Terms," and that was that.[5]

Ownership of the island would have been a simple thing if Cookson would have just paid the land purchase application fee and the purchase price of the island. But on March 15, 1753, when 43 year old Cookson lay dying, he hastily willed the title

The cooling towers at Three Mile Island nuclear power plant. Reactor #2 (left) was built on Joseph Galloway's 1792 land squabble line.

to the island he didn't own to his second wife Mary and his two little daughters from his first marriage, Hannah and Margaret, hoping they could claim it.[6]

Some 18 months later, Cookson's widow married another surveyor and court official, George Stevenson. Little Margaret Cookson died and then in 1760 the surviving heir to two-thirds of the island, Hannah, married the rich Joseph Galloway of Anne Arundel County, Maryland.[7]

Galloway wanted his teenaged wife's two-thirds share of the island right away, not willing to wait a few short years until she turned 21. So one cool September Wednesday in 1762, Hannah's stepmother, and Hannah and her husband watched as the Lancaster County Sheriff and 12 jury men solemnly drew division lines around the shore tracts and the island's upper third.[8]

Galloway's wife now "owned" her share of the unpaid-for island. Galloway now owed the Penns the cost of the island plus fees and also owed Lancaster County the cost of dividing the acreage.[9]

A short nine months later, Galloway's land honeymoon was

over. His new baby and wife Hannah died. Hannah's death transferred her land right to English heirs-in-laws. His fortune might go. He owed the Penns, the Sheriff, and if he wanted his island, he'd owe the English heirs.[10]

It took Galloway and an executor five years to find the heirs and persuade them to sell for fifteen hundred pounds sterling. Galloway was spiraling into a pit of debt. He borrowed the money to pay the heirs, then sold the island and other parcels to an Indian trader named Elliot. The deal was to be completed when the title to the island was presented to Elliot before second payment.[11]

To make a long story short, Galloway couldn't produce the title and was forced to return the Indian trader's money until he could make good by producing the title.[12]

Twenty four years later, after fighting in the Revolutionary War, Galloway was still broke. On June 7, 1798, the Land Office took Indian trader Elliot's money for themselves and gave Elliot's son the island.

For the next 99 years, the Elliot heirs to the island fought among themselves. Debt, greed, deceit, early and unexpected death, picked off various family members, leaving the island's fate in the hands of the court; executors fighting heirs; heirs fighting executors.[13]

Old gentleman farmer James Duffey, who owned that little one-third island section finally acquired the whole island headache in November 1879.

Things were relatively quiet for a few years, that is until March 8, 1904. That year a river of ice, water and mud literally crushed his island and his pocket book. He brought suit against the York Haven Water and Power Company who's dam he believed caused the river to be diverted out of it's normal flow. Then he handed the deed to the first person who would buy it.[14]

Two intense state Supreme Court trials and seven years later, Duffey was awarded just $11,900 in damages.[15] Deceit raised it's ugly head again, making the court awarded damages a pretty bitter pill to take when testimony revealed the electric company duped Duffey. It was their disguised agent who'd lifted the island off his hands.[16]

A few years later, on March 10, 1910, the power company's

farmer tenant, Jacob Landis, experienced the misfortune that was becoming quite common to those associated with the island.

The new hired farm hand's family, the Sonnons, was moving into the lower island farm. Landis and his sons waited at the landing for a load of household goods, some mules, and Mrs. Sonnon and four of their six children. Everything was loaded onto the barge. No sooner had they left their mooring than they found the current too violent to risk crossing. Trying to get back to shore, suddenly the guard rail broke and Landis, 62, disappeared into the churning water. Within a few minutes, the men and four children were overboard; only Mrs. Sonnon still clung to the barge. Result: Jacob Landis, age 62, missing and presumed drowned; Grace, age 9, Carrie age 4, and baby David, age 1 rescued from a raging river; Jacob Jr. age 3, dead.[17]

On Friday, April 1, 22 days later, the body of Jacob Landis was found lodged between two boulders. Mrs. Landis identified him by the handkerchief she knew her husband always wore around his neck.[18]

Sixty-nine years later-to the day-President Jimmy Carter was escorted over that tragic channel on his way to inspect an equally crippled nuclear plant.[19]

One may think that once York Haven owned the island, there would be no more trips to the judge ... not so.[20]

... York Haven put in another dam on the island's east side. Farmer Rider went to the judge to keep the east channel water for his shore crops. Result: York Haven had to blow out the dam.[21]

... York Haven back into court about school taxes for the island's little yellow schoolhouse-ownership meant protection from suits, not education for kids. Result: York Haven: won, children: zero.[22]

York Haven then sold their generating rights to Metropolitan Edison, and guess what? Metropolitan Edison put their nuclear reactor Number 2, right, smack-dab on top of Joseph Galloway's 1792 honeymoon island, land-squabble boundary line.[23]

... and then it was March again, March 28, 1979, and Number 2 reactor belched radioactive death into the air ... and the whole world noticed.

By the way, Three Mile Island was back into court again. This time, the people wanted to bury it. After six years and six months, the Supreme Court said "no."[24] The island was back in operation, and we know the rest . . . or do we?

Author's note: Philip Guedalla* (1889-1944) once wrote: "History repeats itself; historians repeat each other."[25] His statement may hold true most of the time. But in the case of Elaine Huber, historian, genealogist, and researcher, from who's work this story was based, he couldn't be further from the truth.

A former high school and college English teacher, her research into the island's background has stretched over eight years. Each tiny bit of information she has amassed is meticulously documented, and crossed referenced. Large binder notebooks are filled with information, transparencies, deeds and other official documents. Three by five index cards hold bits of information, which at last count numbered 13,000.

Her work has allowed her to paint a detailed and interesting portrait of very human, real people, who lived and died over the last 250 years. A true story of deceit, deception, and greed has turned the history of Three Mile Island into a truth stranger than fiction.

Her wealth of research about the yet unwritten history is scheduled for future publication. I'm sure it will prove to be a unique, colorful, and interesting account.

*Guedalla was a successful biographer and non-repetitive historian.

The Enchanted Garden at the Rail Road House

Is it the soft fluttering of butterfly wings, or the cool, summer breezes that drift and swirl among the lavender, that beckon the lovely lady beyond the garden wall? Is she searching for a lost love, a lost moment in time, or a memory linked to the stately brick tavern known as the Rail Road House?

No one seems to know for sure, but she has popped in and drifted out of the mansion's garden several times in the last few years.

The object of her affection may never be known. Is it possible her appearance may be linked to the sprawling, brick building that stands at the corner of West Front and South Perry Streets in the sleepy little village of Marietta?

The Rail Road House Restaurant and Bed and Breakfast is a charming place even without it's enchanted garden. Built about 1820 to service the bustling canal trade, the hotel became a haven for nineteenth century rivermen.

Rick and Donna Chambers, who bought the old hotel in 1989, told of its colorful past: "Colonel Thomas Scott was the most famous owner of the place. We have his old letterhead paper and wine bills and such. We think he was the president of the Pennsylvania Rail Road; we're not positive on that point, but old rail road records indicate that a Colonel Thomas Scott held that job and we think he is the same person. That conclusion makes sense because the rail road station across the street, that is part of the property, was built by a local rail road company. That private company was started by James Buchanan, Simon Cameron, and Colonel Thomas Scott around 1860, the same dates that appear

The Rail Road House as it appeared sometime prior to 1880. Built originally to service canal workers it is still a restaurant and hotel. Photo courtesy of Rick and Donna Chambers.

on our former owner's wine and food receipts. The station itself was closed down as a stop on the Pennsylvania Rail Road shortly after World War II, but remains virtually unchanged. There is still 1860 graffiti on the walls written in tar."

The hotel itself remains pretty much as it was 180 years ago. One interesting alteration, which reflects changing social attitudes, is the removal of a wall which split the dining room. This brick wall sliced the very large, yet cozy room in half. One side had two fireplaces; the other side had none. Years ago, on a frigid, wintry night, only the rich customers enjoyed the crackling fires. The common working man sat on the other side of the wall, eating his fare and chipping his frozen beer out of his mug. Today all dinner guests can enjoy the dancing flames.

When you visit the hotel and restaurant for dinner or a vacation stay—don't expect to get the pants scared off you, it probably won't happen. It is only the lucky few who dine in the garden on summer evenings who may catch a glimpse of the Victorian bell.

The guest rooms, which are beautifully furnished with period antiques, are relatively quiet, except for the one. Working in this room one evening, the owner was startled to hear the sharp crack of musket fire. One could speculate and say it might have been an echo from the past when barroom brawls and "Ladies of the Evening" frequented the establishment.

Donna, the owner, says, "I walk all over the place at anytime of the day or wee hours of the morning and have never seen anything ... well, not a ghost anyway. We sometimes hear footsteps pacing across the dining room floor when we are in the cellar tavern ... even our three year old daughter has no fear of the place."

... and then there is Ann Marie, who lived next door, about 135 years ago.

She has been spotted on and off in the hotel's garden many times over the decades. Her ghostly appearances have never been such a "big deal" with the locals. Rick and Donna found that out, shortly after opening for business in 1989.

Donna's husband, Rick continued: "I have never seen her but our former chef did ... that was about 1989. He was a bit shook up when it happened. A lot of our customers are locals and have been coming here for years. I just happened to mention to one diner that the chef had quite a scare out in the garden one evening. They just smiled and chuckled and said, 'Oh, that's just Anne Marie, she's been haunting that garden for years. Lived next door to your place you know. Likes to pick flowers, ... wears an old fashion Victorian dress with a large brimmed hat, has a soft glow around her ... s'been dead for a long time ... yep ... that's Ann Marie.'"

The most recent sighting was last summer in 1994. Donna explains: "Kim Harmes worked as a waitress for us last summer. She hadn't heard about the ghost because she had just started working here ... and Kim came in here off the patio just flippin' out. It was a very warm night and she said all of sudden she just felt this cold go all through her, and then she saw a presence that glowed ... out in the garden. Kim was really spooked ... really spooked out."

Donna continued to explain that Kim must be pretty special because "Ann Marie" almost exclusively appears to just men. Kim is the only female, that they know of, that has even seen her.

The garden at the Rail Road House in Marietta where ghostly "Ann Marie" has made many appearances over the years.

She hasn't made an appearance lately, not even during last year's Spook-tacular Weekend Ghost Tours. Of course, the weather in October may be just a little too cool for her to stroll the garden. Who knows ... maybe at this year's Ghost Tour Weekend "Ann Marie" will come over the garden wall for a short stroll through the lavender.

Top Hat and Tails

The little town of Marietta still retains its quaint charm of a by-gone era. Caroline Stark, a Marietta native, vividly recalls the day when she may have glimpsed into the shadows of a time long past.

The town was once a busy port for the barges which floated up and down the Susquehanna River, canals, and for the freight which traveled the rails of the Pennsylvania Railroad. Those bustling days are long gone. What remains are the stately mansions, once home to wealthy businessmen and their families who relished the finer things in life. The visitor can still see the lovely mansions occupying their nineteenth century places along clean, well kept and tree-lined streets.

During the eighteen hundreds, the upper crust often times entertained friends and business associates in their stately homes. Guests, decked out in their finery, arrived by carriage for an evening of fine cuisine and entertainment. When the last cigar was smoked, the last bourbon tasted, the last story told, the evening would draw to a close as candles flickered, or gas-lights dimmed. But did all the guests leave so many years ago? Maybe one affair in the Marietta Square still has a guest . . .

The year was about 1946. Caroline, about 16 years old at the time, was accompanying her six year old cousin to the Marietta Movie Theatre located along Market Street.

Those, who have taken a youngster to a movie, know the attention span of a child can sometimes be very short. This was the case with Caroline's little cousin.

The child, whether bored with the movie or just contrary, informed her older chaperone that she was going to leave, and leave she did. This sent the 16 year old Caroline scrambling out

The Marietta Movie Theatre located on Market Street. Photo courtesy of Rick and Donna Chambers and Steve Bailey of Marietta.

of her seat and through the lobby door. Catching up with the headstrong child they continued their homeward journey north on Market Street walking toward the town square.

That's when Caroline saw something she remembers to this day. There on the corner of Gay Street, walking in and out of the three towering trees that lined the Market Street curb, was a man.

She described him: "He was dressed in a black tuxedo and wore a black, silk top hat. Over his shoulders was draped a black cape lined in scarlet silk and he was carrying a black walking stick. His manner I would compare to that of a wind-up toy soldier, but his movements were not jerky, but smooth as silk. Every step he took was precisely the same measured step as the one before, and precisely the same measured step as the one after."

Frightened by his odd dress and his smooth figure-eight movement in and out of the three trees, she quickly grabbed her little cousin's hand and pulled her across the street. She watched the man with frightened, curious interest as they crossed the square. She continued her study of the man as they walked by the corner and up the street.

"I didn't draw my little cousin's attention to the man because I

The Square in Marietta. The three trees were situated along the white fence (center) close to the curb, where a man in top hat and tails paced between them in a figure eight.

didn't want to scare her, I often wish I would have, for I'm sure she would have seen him too," recalled Caroline.

She continued, "I studied the man carefully, for a long time. I would say he was tall and very handsome. The people who lived in the house behind the three trees were very wealthy and often entertained. My initial conclusion was that the strange man was a magician attending a party, but his gait was so strangely out of the ordinary—I dismissed that explanation. And then there was the red-lined cape, that was blowing out behind him. The scarlet lining flashed a sharp contrast to the back tuxedo. That evening there wasn't the slightest hint of a breeze; so why was his cape billowing like that?"

Caroline spoke with conviction: "He was not a vapor or transparent, he was solid. I studied him for quite sometime—I definitely saw him."

Many years later Caroline happened to mention seeing the formally attired stranger to a friend who lived on the Marietta Square, across the street from the tree fronted mansion. The friend seemed rather shocked at her story, but not that shocked.

It wasn't the first time she had heard this gentleman described. Apparently many years ago, a neighbor girl who returned from a date in the early morning hours, was dropped off at the square right across the street from the three trees. She waved goodby to her escort and turned to walk home. What she saw and described was the same fashionably, yet a hundred years out-of-style, attired man.

The stately trees which once shaded the Market Street and Gay Street corner have long since disappeared. The brick walk is now warmed by the afternoon sun.

Who knows, maybe some day, someone else may see the handsome stranger as he paces a figure-eight beneath the boughs of some long forgotten towering trees.

Uncommon Knowledge

How many of us can say with certainty, without a shadow of a doubt, that we are going to live to be very old? Usually the hour of our appointed death is unknown. The only thing we humans know for sure is that it will happen some day, sometime; for it is a full-circle completion of the cycle of life.

One Lancaster woman had that knowledge. Her name was Bessie Irene Schiefer and this is her story.

My memory of Bessie goes back forty years. She and her daughter, Eldora, often came to visit my grandmother, who was Bessie's first cousin.

The visits always proved to be lively with conversation. Politics was a hot topic. A staunch Republican, Bessie had voted in every primary and general election since women got the right to vote in 1920.

I recall, Bessie had a very curious answer to a very ordinary question. When Grandmother asked: "How are you?" Bessie would always reply, "I'm just fine Mabel, you know, I'll always be just fine."

Both would nod at each other with a mutual understanding which was rooted in a near death experience so many years ago.

Bessie entered the world in the stormy and unpredictable month of March, the fourteenth day, 1893. Her home was a frame house along the main street of Mountville, a small community situated between Lancaster and Columbia.

Childhood survival in that century was never a sure thing. Whooping cough, diptheria, pneumonia, occasional small pox outbreaks and a variety of other ailments took their toll on the community, especially the very young.

At age two and a half, Bessie contracted spinal meningitis and hovered near death for many weeks. When asked many years later about her survival she would reply: "It was the whiskey ... my grandmother and the whiskey. She saved me and the whiskey saved me."

The illness left her with a slightly twisted hip and periodic spasms or "fits." The old country doctor who cared and worried over her during her illness, decided to keep a watchful eye on his convalescing patient. For quite a few years she went on rounds with the doctor. In the spring and summer, she rode with him in his buggy as he visited patients. In the winter, she rode with him in the sleigh.

Her next brush with death came in the winter of 1918. Bessie was 25 years old and very pregnant with her first child. An influenza epidemic struck the area and people were dropping like flies. Bessie contracted the flu and sunk into a coma. She remained unconscious for a week.

When she awoke, she had a fantastic tale to tell. "I was in the most beautiful place," she told her mother, "... a place filled with light, and beautiful flowers. I saw the Savior and I was with the angels."

Bessie maintained from that day on, that she would live a long, long time. She would tell everyone that she had already spent a week in heaven and she knew she wasn't supposed to go back for many years to come. The angels told her so.

This knowledge was a very special thing but it failed to ease her grief many years later, after the death of her mother.

Her daughter, Eldora Schiefer, tells about Bessie's strange visitor: "Mother was inconsolable after her mother died. Months had passed and still Mother cried ... she was grief stricken. Then one day, something strange happened. Mom (Bessie) was sitting in the living room sobbing, when the front door opened up and in walked her mother. She came right over to the chair and Mom (Bessie) put her hand out, placing it around the fleshy, top part of her departed mother's arm. Her mother then spoke to her saying: 'Now Bessie, I want you to stop your grieving. It's awful cold in that cemetery; you don't have to come up there to see me. There there, now ... stop your grieving.' Mom felt so much relief after that happened. It truly helped."

Bessie's visit to heaven remained fresh in her mind till the end

Bessie Irene Brown Schiefer (kneeling left) poses with her first cousin Mabel Powers Struck (standing right) and Mabel's future husband (far right) William Eicker Burtz, Sr. and unidentified friends circa 1919.

of her earthly stay. She is fondly remembered by many as a lovely lady with a sparkling intellect. For decades to come, visitors to the Harrisburg state capital can see her name in the Voter's Hall of Fame.

Parts of her will forever linger in Lancaster. Pennsylvania Dutch Country visitors who dine at the Lapp Family Restaurant (formerly Joe Myers' restaurant) can sample their famous Bacon

Salad Dressing. It is Bessie's original recipe, she was head cook at the restaurant for 18 years.

Bessie passed away on October 25, 1992. She was just a few months shy of being one century old.

My husband, sister and I attended her funeral that cold and blustery day in October and paid our last respects. I couldn't help but think that in Bessie's case, the mystery of the after-life was solved.

Where did Bessie go? She, beyond a shadow of a doubt, had a date with an angel.

Author's note: Bessie's death did not prevent her from voting in the 1992 presidential election. She voted by absentee ballot—a Republican to the very end—for George Bush.

Pennsylvania Pow Wow Doctors

Just about everyone who is native to the central Pennsylvania area knows about them. Nobody talks about them. Pow Wow doctors are the seldom discussed subject.

Pow Wowing is the "art of healing by prayer" or the "laying on of hands."[1]

"Pow Wowing goes back ages and ages, though it has no fixed methods, nor has there ever been any cult or group organization established for its promulgation. It is a genuine hand-me-down if ever there was one," wrote A. Monroe Aurand in his book entitled *The Pow-Wow Book*.[2]

During the time I was collecting material for my first book, I received a call from a Strasburg woman. She explained that many years ago she read a newspaper article featuring a man who was writing a book about Pow Wowing. The author requested input from Lancaster area residents to help in his research.

She had intended to call the man because her grandmother was a Pow Wow doctor. The Strasburg woman, whether hesitant to break tradition or just not following through with her intent to make the telephone call, did not contact the author.

The woman told me that sometime later, the newspaper reported the intended book was abandoned. The struggling writer had received no response from anyone in the Pennsylvania Dutch Country.

One of the earliest books written about the art was published on July 31, 1819 near Reading, Berks County, Pa. Johann Georg Hohmann titled his book Der Lang Verbogene Freund or "The

Long Lost Friend." First published in German, the first English translation printing appeared in 1855.

The Long Lost Friend offered cures, protections and preventative measures. These "prescriptions" were and still are deeply entwined with scripture and superstition.

The ability to stop bleeding and the pain of burns was often mentioned as two of the noted abilities of the Pow Wow doctors.

For instance, John Georg Hohmann's *The Long Lost Friend* gives instructions "to stop bleeding at any time":

> Write the name of the four principal waters of the whole world, glowing out of Paradise, on a paper, namely: Pison, Gihon, Hedekiel and Pheat, and put it on the wound. In the first book of Moses, the second chapter, verses 11, 12, 13, you will find them. You will find this effective.[3]

> Another Way To Stop Blood
> As soon as you cut yourself you must say: "Blessed wound, blessed hour, blessed be the day on which Jesus Christ was born, in the name of the Father, Son, and Holy Ghost. Amen.[4]

> Another Similar Presentation
> Breathe three times upon the patient, and say the Lord's Prayer three times until the words, "upon the earth," and the bleeding will be stopped.[5]

Hohmann's prescription to take the "fire" out of a burn goes as follows:

> Clear out, brand but never in; be thou cold or hot, thus must cease to burn. May God guard thy blood and thy flesh, thy marrow and thy bones, and every artery, great and small. They all shall be guarded and protected in the name of God against inflammation and mortification, in the name of God the Father, Son and Holy Ghost. Amen.[6]

My own family, who's roots go back to Germany, over the years have exhibited some practices which seem to have their origins in old healing practices.

Grandfather had suffered from hearing loss for many years. The condition progressed quickly and left him nearly totally deaf. Local doctors, as well as Philadelphia specialists, were consulted; but the diagnosis was the same. His condition was caused by nerve death, no medical doctor could help.

It was at that time, after all conventional methods were exhausted, that Grandfather visited a Pow Wow doctor. My father summed up his personal opinion of the "office visit." His statement contained a few more colorful explicatives which I won't print. Father bellowed: "That quack charged Pop twenty bucks to blow in his ears with a broom straw. He still was as deaf as a stone!"

Needless to say, Dad seemed to be just a teeny, weeny, bit doubtful about faith healers and Pow Wow doctors. But that didn't stop him from "dosing" my sisters and I with sweet oil.

Cuts, burns, bruises, boils and infected ears were all treated with this sweet smelling unguent. I often wondered if my late father knew that sweet oil was named in Hohmann's Pow Wow prescriptions.

Hohmann writes:

> "Sweet oil possesses a great many valuable properties, and it is therefore advisable for every head of family to have it at all times about the house in order that it may be applied in cases of necessity."

It was a remedy for: "inflammation in men and animals, internally and externally. It also was recommended to treat heartburn, poisoning, snake bites, rabid dog bites, dysentery, internal injuries from falls, all swellings and burns.[7]

Superstition and hex signs were used by our family over a century ago. Great Great Grandfather Keppler built our home in 1868 (the house was featured in Haunted Lancaster County Pennsylvania, "The Girls Of Kinderhook", in 1994). Educated at the University of Heidelburg prior to his immigrating to the United States in 1856, his intellect reserved a corner for superstition.

He and his wife were very familiar with the protective qualities attributed to "hex" signs. Our living room ceiling, under several layers of old wallpaper, is painted a cobalt blue. In the center of the ceiling is a giant, eight pointed star enclosed in a circle. It measures three and a half feet in diameter, and is painted a bright yellow.

Whether it was intended to protect against evil spirits or fire, we do not know. It remains as it was painted 125 years ago. It has worked this long, why tamper with "protective" success?

Many may be skeptics, especially in this day of innovation and invention. One Columbia man, George White, is not so much the sceptic since his encounter with a Pow Wow doctor and physic from Allentown.

It happened about 14 years ago while he was in Allentown installing awnings for a resident. Mr. White explained:

"The installation was an all day job. I had noticed during the day's work that large cars were pulling up to the residence and well dressed women were going into the house. There was a lot of traffic going in and out. When the job was finished I knocked on the door. Some ladies were cooking inside and they invited me in. I glanced around and noticed there were religious crucifixes on the wall.

Then an older blind man came out of the other room. He was the man who must have contracted the job and he paid for awning. Then, out of the clear blue sky, he said, 'Bring your mother up. I can help her. She has a heart condition . . . somebody is talking about you and your cousin playing baseball.'"

Mr. White was a little taken back by the blind man's statements. He drove back to Lancaster and got home about 7PM. Rather curious about the day, he asked his mother (who indeed did have a heart condition) if she had company that day.

She replied, "Why yes, Aunt Helen was here. We were talking about you boys (meaning his cousin) playing baseball."

Mr. White forgot about the unusual meeting until sometime later when his daughter was experiencing medical problems. George White transformed before my eyes, as the conversation about the "apple-of-his-eye" brought a soft glow to his face. He explained how she was born retarded. Over the years, her health had been of great concern to him and his wife.

His daughter was having a bad time of it. She was extremely agitated and restless and was not sleeping at night. Her doctors had no answers and he and his wife were very worried.

That is when Mr. White remembered the blind man who had offered to help his mother. He and his daughter drove to Allentown.

George White tells about the meeting:

"The first thing the Pow Wow doctor said was 'your wife doesn't believe I can help or she would be here too.' Then he said that my daughter should change her diet. She was not to eat nuts—walnuts were for squirrels. She was also to stop eating the fruit she was eating for a couple of weeks. He said he would pray for her."

Within three days his daughter showed marked improvement. She started to sleep through the night, much to the relief of Mr. and Mrs. White. His daughter continues to do well.

Pow-Wowing was and is still practiced. A. Monroe Aurand touches on just how widespread the practice was in the 1920's when he interviewed a local medical doctor from York County who said: "In case of hemorrhage from the nose, from a wound or from other cause, a common cure is to wrap a red woolen string round each finger; another is to lay an axe under the bed, edge upward; and you can't talk them (his local patients) out of it. I used to get angry when I first came here, but I found that it was of no use. These are not occasional things only, but I have seem them over and over again. Then there are prayers for stopping blood, always in 'Dutch'. They can't be sick in English, and the first question to me as a physician has been 'Kansht du Deutsch'? (Do you speak German?)[8]

Pow-Wowing is intricately interwoven with religion and scripture. The Bible is filled with stories of Jesus healing the sick. John XIV, 12—"He that believeth in me, the works that I do shall he do also."

Also in James V, 14—"Is any sick among you? Let him call (the Lord) and the prayer of faith shall save the sick."[9]

Physicians have been known to give placebos or medicines which scientifically have no healing benefits. Many times the patient, convinced that the "medicine" will cure him, recovers. The patient healed himself. The placebo bolstered his "faith" in the physician, his "faith" in the cure (the placebo), and created a positive mental attitude in which recovery was expected and attained.

In the last few years, universities have been conducting studies exploring the effect prayer has on the recovery of the sick. Much to the surprise of the scientific community, those sick who were prayed for, had a higher recovery rate than those individuals who were not.

Medical treatments for sickness and injury have changed

constantly over the centuries. Advanced technology and scientific discoveries have revolutionized medicine. No physician today would "bleed" a dying patient, which was standard treatment in the 1700's in the United States. No physician today would "cup" a patient, a treatment still practiced by some into the twentieth century.

Some treatments have just gone out of style. For instance, pneumonia and some respiratory infections were once treated with mustard plasters. Dry mustard was mixed with water and the resulting paste was then spread on pieces of linen or cloth. The cloth was then placed on the chest for a variable amount of time; the concoction generated heat and produced a drawing effect, so a watchful eye was kept to prevent burning of the skin.

Many years ago, after exhausting all modern treatment for my nasty case of viral pneumonia, a local doctor suggested mustard plasters and sunshine. Reluctant to prescribe such treatment and doubtful of its effectiveness, his new method of medical attack was in addition to the "wonder drugs."

After six weeks of feeling as if I was at death's door, and wondering if the doctor was going to pull me through, I was ready to try anything. I basked in the sun like a beached whale and on a regular basis, applied the sloppy mustard plasters. Also during this time my family spent an inordinate amount of time praying for me.

Within ten days the pneumonia was gone. Was it the "wonder drugs", the sun, the mustard plasters, or the prayer that influenced my recovery? Or was it just the faith I had in a small town doctor who dared to try an old remedy that years ago had "gone out of style"?

Today, Pennsylvania Pow Wowers still practice, if one knows where to find them; but they are a dying breed. Today for most local residents it is alright to get sick in "English". Some of the remedies and cures of the Pow Wower have been forgotten or just aren't used anymore. However, the basic ingredient, the iron web, into which the cures and superstitions are woven remains strong and intact. It is called faith; and faith in God never goes out of style.

Who Are You Going to Call?

Getting "slimed" was a sure indication of a ghost in the hit movie *Ghost Busters*. The ghost hunters in this film were called to rid haunted sites of their ghostly inhabitants. They arrived wearing highly technical equipment strapped to their backs which closely resembled canister vacuum cleaners. After an exciting, coordinated ectoplasmic isolation procedure, the entities were sucked up, removed, and placed in storage.

The film, of course, was fiction. The canister vacuum cleaners that I am familiar with have trouble picking up a wispy piece of white lint off a red carpet, let alone sucking up a ghost.

Who is to say, however, that getting "slimed" is fiction? One Willow Street family got "slimed" and they attribute it to their resident ghosts.

George, Sandy, their two sons, several household pets, and three ghosts all share the same house. Their home is relatively new in construction, not a Victorian "Lady" or a log cabin often found in Lancaster County. The house doesn't have a long history which often times is connected with a ghostly inhabitant.

The family moved into their home in June of 1979. According to Sandy, for the first 10 years the strange occurrences were sporadic, but by 1991, so many things had happened, she started keeping a written record of the events.

She kindly provided me with a copy of her journal in 1993; and sent me an updated version in 1995. Because of her kindness I am able to share the family's experiences with you as the events appear in her journal. For readability I will condense some of the frequently re-occurring events.

The evidence suggests their home is inhabited by a poltergeist. Poltergeists are a very ancient psychic manifestation, having appeared in all parts of the world and with every race of people. The word is German meaning "noisy spirit." For hundreds of years people believed that they were evil spirits amusing themselves by tormenting living persons. Famed Nador Fodor, after years of study of poltergeists, concluded that they were some form of vital energy radiated from a living body. He said they appeared to be a bundle of emotions, with a directive mind, split off from a body.[1]

Poltergeists have rung bells, turned light switches on and off, broken dishes, moved heavy objects around, dropped hot stones inside closed rooms. These stones, when marked and thrown into a river, were soon back in the house. They have tied knots in clothing and turned wine into ink. They have driven families from their homes and done almost everything impossible that can be imagined.[2]

Sandy, George, and their family have no intention of leaving. They like their home, and they like the ghosts who make life a little more interesting.

Sandy writes: "Everything I have written is true. We came to a conclusion about everything I've written about that it wasn't earthly or human, although at the beginning my husband tried to make up excuses when there were none."

Her careful record keeping allowed Sandy to conclude: ". . . (The most activity) happens toward the end of the months, through the beginning of the next month."

The family's household pets sense something strange in the house and aren't afraid to growl their disapproval. The two dogs and the cat have favorite spots in the house where they growl at an invisible intruder.

Sandy writes: ". . . (our dogs and cat) growl at the wall at the bottom of the cellar steps and at the wall behind the cellar steps. On lots of occasions they will either growl or bark at the kitchen wall. On lots of occasions the trash can lid will swing all by itself. No one puts anything in it for a long time. It just decides to swing back and forth."

Barking and growling at particular walls or following some invisible occupant of the room with their eyes, Sandy describes their pet's eye movements as similar to a dog or cat watching the movements of a fly. There is only one problem, there is no fly, no bee, no nothing. This happens so frequently she has given up writing down every time it happens.

Back in 1991 she watched in amazement as one leafy strand of her Boston fern moved back and forth for a full minute. No other part of the plant or pot was disturbed. There was no wind, no draft, no breeze.

November 1991: "This one happened at the end of the month. We can't explain this one at all. I had purchased a wall-hanging from a House of Lloyd party and wanted to put it up at the end of our hall. George was putting it up. He was hammering or putting screws into the wall when he noticed a wet, slimy substance between his two fingers. He showed me and I jokingly told him 'he got slimed'. There was nothing in the wall or anywhere where he could have gotten slimy fingers. About a half hour later he heard a clanging sound in our bedroom which sounded like aluminum pie pans banging together. We both investigated and found nothing.

December 1991: "The boys and I went bowling Friday night. George (her husband) was sleeping in our bedroom. The dog was penned up in the kitchen. George woke up and heard something like someone jumping on John's (their son) bed. He thought John was home and yelled for John to stop. He got no answer and got out of bed because he heard it again. When he got to John's room he saw no one and didn't hear the noise. He went back to bed and heard the noise again. He didn't get back out of bed."

April 19, 1992: "I was sitting in John's bedroom looking toward the north side of the house watching the hamsters play. John's dresser is towards the south wall of his bedroom, when all of a sudden his money started falling out of his wallet. It startled me and I looked around thinking John was there but no one was there."

July (?), 1992: "I had wash in the dryer and had the dryer on. I went to the store to get something and when I got back I thought it shouldn't be dry yet because I wasn't gone that long. I opened the dryer door, the clothes were still damp. I looked up at the gray fuse box and the lever was pushed to off. It could not have fallen down because it is hard to push up or down. Who threw the switch?"

Sandy has also found her washer stopped in the middle of a wash cycle. Some one lifted the washer lid preventing the machine from going into the rinse cycle. No one in the house did this, and Sandy doesn't interrupt her machine once it is started. Most women don't.

Along with all the growling pets, Sandy and her family experience things falling off shelves and flying off walls. One of the strangest things happened while they were away on vacation in 1993. They didn't learn about it until they returned and found the batteries of their smoke alarms placed on the kitchen table. Sandy's parents explained the situation and it was then entered in her journal.

February 2, 1993: "My parents came up around 6:30 PM to check on our house. Mom stayed in the car, and Dad came in the house and turned the kitchen light on. Suddenly the smoke alarm came on in the kitchen. He stopped and stood still and the alarm stopped. He moved and it came on. He went out to tell Mom to witness it. She came in and stood inside the kitchen door and he showed her what happened. He then turned on the living room light. As soon as he stepped into the living room the smoke alarm in the hall started. Every time he would stop, both alarms would stop. He stood right underneath the alarm in the hall and it made the shrillest noise. He didn't check the bedrooms after that. He removed the battery from the kitchen alarm."

February 4, 1993, 7:00 PM: "My parents came to check the house again. Smoke alarm in the hall did the same thing. Dad said he heard the smoke alarm as he got out of the car. Dad put the battery back in the one in the kitchen. Both alarms behaved the way they did the other day when my parents checked the house. Dad pulled the battery on the one in the hall and put it on the kitchen table. That is where we found them when we returned home from vacation. If they were alarming since February 2, solid, the batteries would have been worn out. We told our ghost before we left on the 29th of January to watch over the house, but we forgot to mention someone was coming to check the house. Instead of guard dogs, we have a guard ghost."

The family is also awakened at night by loud noises. They have had items disappear and then just as mysteriously, show up again. Sandy and George sometimes are awakened at night by their bed shaking. It rocks back and forth for 2 to 3 seconds, then everything is still. They still can't figure that one out.

They also have a problem with lights turning on and off by themselves. The cellar door has a mind of its own, it opens and closes by itself. The door knob must be turned though but that doesn't prevent it from happening totally unattended.

The family aren't the only ones who have witnessed the ghosts. Imagine the surprise one house guest got as they used the bathroom facilities and heard some one clearing their throat in the shower. No magazines in that room.

Sandy had been convinced for a long time that the house was haunted. Her husband, George, was skeptical. That is until the fire alarm incident. How do you talk to a ghost? Sandy thought she would try a Ouija Board.

October 13, 1994: "These questions are not in order. We asked the same questions several times and most of the time we got the same answers. A lot of abbreviations were used in the answers although we can't figure some things (answers) out."

We first asked if anyone was here?	Yes
What is the name?	W.A.W.
What does the W. mean?	WILL
William?	Yes
Did you die in this house?	No
Did you die near here?	Yes
What year did you die?	1922
1922?	Yes
Do you live in the basement?	Yes
Are you evil?	No
Did our dog see you?	Yes
In the laundry room?	Yes
What year were you born?	1848
Are you still here?	Yes
Do you still live in the house?	Yes
How many other ghosts live here?	3
Do you have a wife?	yes

What is her name?	MAR
Mary?	Yes
How did you die?	M N M
What does M N M mean?	(nothing)M N M
Did you smoke?	NO
How long have you been here?	10 Years
How long have you lived here?	39 Years
Are you an Indian?	Yes
Are you Cheroke?	Yes
Are you Susquehannock?	No
How many kids do you have?	No
Do you have any adopted kids?	Yes
Do you have a son?	Yes
How old is he?	10 Years
Did you have any pets?	CAT
What is your last name?	WAY
WAY?	Yes
Is your name William Way?	Yes
What is your middle name?	ALG
Did you die of natural causes?	Yes
Did you commit suicide?	No
How old are you?	49

(Sandy then asked what ages the people in the room were. According to Sandy the board operators couldn't have faked these answers, but the responses were correct.)

What animal did we have that died?	CAT

(Their cat did die.)

Did you scare my dad with the smoke alarm when we were in Florida?	Yes
What is my dad's name?	R.L.

(Sandy says this is correct. The board operators could not have known this.)

April 2, 1995 Ouija Board was used again:

What is the first initial of your first name?	J
Is it Jimmy?	No
Is it Jake?	No
Is it Jack?	Yes
What is the first initial of your last name?	G
Can you spell your last name?	GEER
How old are you?	9

Do you have brothers or sisters here?	No
Do you have a Mom and Dad here?	No
Are you adopted?	Yes
Do you live here?	Yes
So you live here with William?	Yes
What year did you die?	No response
How old is William?	48
Did you move the phone cord?	Yes
How long have you lived here?	7 years
Do you like living here with us?	Yes

As stated before, most of the family doesn't fear whatever is causing the strange occurrences. The dog, however, shakes with fear quite often and refuses to enter certain rooms or refuses to enter the house occasionally.

John, one of the sons, is a bit spooked by the whole thing. This reaction is understandable. John, who is 18, has had several close encounters of the "other kind". Home alone one evening, he was in his bedroom and all of a sudden he heard music. He investigated and found (under his brother's bed) his brother's keyboard was playing. He called his friend to spend the night.

On another occasion, a friend slept over night. The poor fellow woke up because something heavy was sitting on his legs. It was all he could do to stifle a scream. Of course, no one was on his legs, no one was in the room but John who was asleep and the household cat who was curled up at his head near the pillow.

Sandy will probably continue to keep a journal. Who knows what might happen in the future? Just who do you call when you have a few ghosts sharing your house? I'm glad she decided to call me. Maybe I'll stop by someday ... with my vacuum cleaner.

Hempfield Haunting

A farm situated in West Hempfield Township, Lancaster County, has a ghostly inhabitant which walks by elevated windows and in and out of the barn.

I received a phone call from the farm's present owner who told me about their unusual guest.

The stone farmhouse and its adjoining barn dates back to 1795. It is situated not far from Route 23, which in another century was a paved toll road stretching from Philadelphia to Marietta.

The Smith family moved into the 200 year old farm back in 1991. Refurbishing was started immediately after their arrival. The floors were sanded and the interior rooms were painted. The first indication of something out of the ordinary occurred when Mr. Smith heard someone call his name as he painted the ceiling. He dropped his work and went outside to see who it was. No one was there.

That, of course, could happen to anyone. It was forgotten. Work continued.

The dining room was an area where the Smiths spent a lot of time painting. This room had a window which was situated high above outside ground level. A large bush grew tall and bushy and reached to just below the window sill. That is why the Smiths were so alarmed when they saw the black shadow of a person float by that window. Whoever cast that shadow would have to be either ten feet tall or walking on stilts to block out the sun's rays for the shadow to fall in that particular room. Investigation revealed no one.

Others, including Mrs. Smith's sister-in-law, saw the shadow pass. On one such occasion in the dining room, the sister-in-law, accompanied by her pet Rottweiler, were startled by what she described as the shadow of a man in a black trench coat wearing a rounded black hat.

Mrs. Smith explained, "My sister-in-law and her dog went outside to investigate. The dog had his dander up, and was 'gruffing' deep in his throat. When they got outside they then caught a glimpse of a man in a red-plaid flannel shirt walking into the barn. Her dog started growling and took off, fur puffed and spiked, and followed the man into the barn. By that time, I came around the corner. I assured her that I had not been outside the window and that couldn't have been my husband. He was with me."

Mrs. Smith's brother has also seen the man in the red-plaid flannel shirt walking into the barn. He too thought it was Mr. Smith. Investigating, he found no one in the barn, and Mr. Smith was located at some other area of the property.

Other strange things have happened. These include being rousted out of bed at 2AM by loud "pop," "pop," "pops." This caused both Mr. and Mrs. to sit bolt up-right in bed, their hearts aflutter.

In the fall of 1993, while putting shutters on the windows, they heard a terrible crash. It sounded like a plate glass window shattering, but they could find no broken glass. Several days later Mrs. Smith was cleaning the bedroom floor. She picked up the bed's dust ruffle and found that a very large piece of glass had broken . . . under the bed.

Often times, the Smiths hear footsteps walking the upstairs hallway towards their bedroom door. The footsteps stop at the door. They investigate. No one is there.

Mrs. Smith has also been awakened at 5:15 AM by a loud knock at the door. No one is there.

One of the most curious occurrences is the disappearing shirt. Mrs. Smith explained, "My husband wore and still wears work clothing. When he is finished with the job he hangs his work shirt in the cellar-way. That shirt has turned up missing several times. He can't find it. I can't find it. I haven't put it in the wash, but we just have no idea what happened to it. Then we open up the cellar-way and there it is. It reappears. The shirt is back."

Disappearing laundry is not that unusual. Personally, I have a big problem with disappearing socks. I put ten into the washer; I take nine out. I put six in; I take five out. Those missing socks will never be seen again in our life time.

I guess it would be safe to say Mr. Smith's shirt doesn't totally disappear forever while it is missing from its hook in the cellar-way. At least they catch glimpses of the red-plaid flannel shirt every now and then as it goes into the barn.

Odds and Ends, Bits and Pieces

1870 HAUNTING IN YORK COUNTY

The following haunted house story was reported in the Columbia Spy, Saturday, May 21, 1870:

The York Republican is responsible for the following. Probably the Spirit is that of some departed democrat, who is visiting earth to see this XVth Amendment:-"A house on West King street has lately been visited by mysterious sounds, and the heavy tread of invisible footsteps. The unsuspecting inmates were first disturbed by continued pacing to and fro on the sidewalk in front of the house, as if a sentinel was passing over his beat, and on looking out they heard the same steps, but saw no one. Soon the same sounds proceeded from the kitchen, and then up the stairs, and in the bedroom. While the light was burning brightly in the room the unearthly visitor passed through with solemn march. Then groans and sighs proceeded from the corner of the room, as if a being was in unutterable distress, and then the cover was torn from the bed.

Investigations into the mystery have thus far proved unsatisfactory. These supernatural visits were repeated with fearful regularity every night for several weeks after which there was a temporary silence.

The plainest manifestations occurred between one and three o'clock in the morning. A young man who questioned the truth of the affair, a relative of the family residing in the house, made up his mind to pass a night there, in order to see for himself. After he had quietly retired, his doubts were almost confirmed into a decided disbelief, until about one o'clock, when the usual tramp was heard on the front pavement. He says it seems as if a person was walking who had a wooden limb. The gate of the side entrance was securely fastened but without being opened, a few moments afterwards the same pacing was heard on the back porch.

The table in the kitchen commenced moving around as if it has been suddenly changed to a thing of life. The whole family immediately went down to the kitchen but found the table quietly standing at its usual place. Although bright lights were kept lit in the rooms, nothing could be seen while at the same time the tramp of the invisible visitant astonished listeners. Everything connected to this affair remains shrouded in mystery.

---

*The Fourteen and Fifteenth Amendments to the Constitution made citizens of the former slaves and guaranteed the men among them the right to vote.

CEMETERY GHOST

The Lancaster New Era, December 2, 1994 edition reported that the ghost of a Civil War soldier floated out of St. Mary's cemetery and scared the "dickens" out of a Lancaster man.

According to the eye witness, the ghost took a "pot-shot" at him. The incident was reported to police. No hole or bullet was found so the investigating officer did not file a report.

SPOTTED ON A LONELY ROAD

A Lancaster County citizen wrote to tell me of a strange occurrence which happened to a close relative.

Many years ago their relative and a friend were driving home at night in the area of the old Mennonite church and graveyard in Hinkletown.

Both passangers saw a man, crawling on his hands and knees, crossing the road in front of them.

The strange thing was that the passengers could see right through the man's rib cage as the car lights illuminated the ghostly crawler.

Years ago, during the time when cars had running boards, many drivers reported that "something" would jump on the running board about a half mile from the graveyard.

A thump was heard when it hitched the ride. The strange passenger then jumped off with a thump, at the cemetery.

GUARDING A TREASURE

Reeves Goehring of Columbia told me of a strange thing that happened to him in a wooded area in West Hempfield Township.

He was filling buckets of dirt with a shovel, preparing an area for target practice.

For some strange reason, he had one of those strange 'it feels like I'm being watched' feelings. He continued to work for about an hour and a half.

Finally, he couldn't stand it any longer. The hair at the nape of his neck still signaled something out of the ordinary, so he packed it in and left.

Some time later, he happened to mention the strange occurrence to a friend. The friend then told him that an old legend tells of a highway man who was supposed to have hid his booty in that area of West Hempfield. It is said his spirit still walks the woods protecting his buried treasure.

POOF... YOU'RE GONE

It was reported a Lancaster woman spontaneously combusted into a cloud of smoke...

I guess I'll save that story for next time.

So You Want To See A Ghost?

Ghost watching is a whole lot like whale watching ... it's pretty hard to get them to make an appearance on que. Experiencing one on a ghost tour is possible; I found that out on my first Ghost Tour in Gettysburg recently.

I am not a ghost hunter; I just happen to write about ghosts. Curious about the Gettysburg Ghost Tours, four of us made a reservation for a July evening tour.

I was one of a group of eight that moved from stop to stop along the town streets as our costumed guide explained the various points of hauntings. It was the fourth stop on the tour, just across the street from the Farnsworth House Bed and Breakfast, which sticks in my mind. Just as the guide started to speak, I was suddenly very pre-occupied with the very sweet scent of pipe tobacco. I sniffed the air like a blood hound and craned my neck around looking for its source. I even went so far as to move several steps to the right and left trying to get a clear view of the face of the very wide man who had his back turned towards me. I did not want to be rude to our guide by speaking out of turn, but I was so perplexed I turned to my friend and said, "Who's smoking that ..."

Almost at the same moment, our guide, who I have to admit I was ignoring because of the mesmerizing sweet smell of tobacco, said, "... and the lady who lives here says she often smells the sweet scent of ..."

Both of us almost finished in unison: "... pipe tobacco."

At that moment I think our guide needed an ammonia capsule cracked under her nostrils. She looked a little pale. I was rather stumped. No one else smelled it. We were standing down-wind of ... no one.

That is what happened during my very first ghost tour.

HISTORIC MARIETTA
GHOST WALK

Friday-Saturday-Sunday
OCTOBER 27, 28, 29, 1995

The Rail Road House in Historic Marietta presents the annual GHOST WALK in 1995. It is a full weekend event scheduled for:

OCTOBER 27, 28, and 29

Guests enjoy a guided GHOST WALK through Historic Marietta with stops at "haunted places" along the way. Last stop is historic SHANK'S TAVERN (featured in *Haunted Lancaster County: Ghosts and Other Strange Occurrences*, 1994) for a tour and refreshments.

The weekend also features events for
young and old alike . . . hayrides,
wienie roasts, pumpkin carving
old-time horror movies
Masquerade
Halloween Theme Dinner

Sunday Brunch

Last year's event was so successful reservations are suggested:

Call Donna Chambers at
THE RAIL ROAD HOUSE
RESTAURANT & BED AND BREAKFAST
W. Front and S. Perry St., Marietta, Pa. 17547

Dial: (717) 426-4141
FOR INFORMATION ON TOURS, WEEKEND LODGING, SCHEDULE OF EVENTS

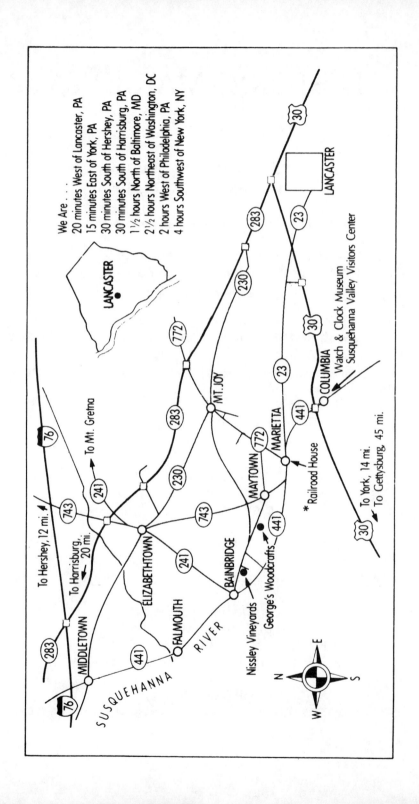

HOW TO GET TO THE RAIL ROAD HOUSE:

FROM POINTS NORTH:

95 South to 287
To Tapanzee Bridge to Garden State Parkway.
To New Jersey Turnpike.
To Pennsylvania Turnpike.
To Route 222 South to Route 30 West.
Exit Route 30 West at the Columbia-Marietta Exit.
Bear Right at the end of the exit to get on 441 North.
Follow 441 North until the first traffic light.
Make a left at the light on to Market Street.
Follow Market Street all the way through the traffic circle.
The first street to the left once you go through the circle is Perry Street.
Make a left onto Perry Street and Rail Road House is at the end of the street.

FROM POINTS SOUTH:

95 North to 695 to 83 North.
To Route 30 East.
Exit Route 30 East at the Columbia-Marietta exit.
At the end of the exit ramp there is a stop sign. Make a right.
Go to the next stop sign and make another right to get on 441 North.
Follow 441 North until the first traffic light.
Make left at the light onto Market.
Follow Market all the way through the traffic circle.
The first street to the left once you go through the circle is Perry Street.
Left on Perry to the end of the block.

Acknowledgements

I would like to thank everyone who has contacted me and shared their special experience or story with me. Without them this book would not be possible.

A special thanks also to those who bought my first book. Your interest and support gave me courage to write this second collection of tales.

Thank you also to my sister, Bette J. Crouse. She is always there to help and advise. She has the uncanny ability to recall obscure information and accurate leads for stories long forgotten.

Thank you Elaine Huber for sharing your extensive research about Three Mile Island with me.

A bushel and a peck to my wonderful husband Sam. He is the one who keeps me focused on 'the next book' and patiently reads all my attempts while wielding the red pen of constructive criticism.

I would also like to thank my critics, who have given new meaning to a phrase coined by Mark Twain: ". . . a pen warmed up in hell." Their remarks had their desired effect. After my blistered fingers healed and I surfaced on the other side of the Atlantic . . . with a verb in my mouth . . . I continued writing with renewed confidence and zest. Alas, my ears were still filled with sea water and I almost didn't hear them whisper: "I knew Mark Twain . . . and he you ain't," as I dutifully plugged away at the 'ol word processor.

Thank you. Thank you very much.

FOOTNOTES

Science and Shadows

1. John Bartlett, Edited by Emily Morris Beck and the editorial staff of Little, Brown and Company, *Bartlett's Familiar Quotations* (Boston and Toronto: Little, Brown and Company, 1980). 921.

2. Corinne McLaughlin & Gordon Davidson, "Divine Guidance Behind America's Founding," *Venture Inward,* November/December 1994, 23.

3. Ibid.

4. Ibid.

5. Ibid.

6. General George Washington, and Marvin Kitman, *George Washington's Expense Account* (Simon and Schuster, 1970; repr., New York: Harper & Row, 1988), 31.

7. J. T. Fraser, *Time The Familiar Stranger* (Amherst: The University of Massachusetts Press, 1987), 14.

8. Ibid.

9. Richard Morris, *Time's Arrows: Scientific Attitudes Toward Time* (New York: Simon and Schuster, 1985), 209.

10. By the Editors of Time-Life Books, *Time and Space: Mysteries of The Unknown* (Alexandria, Virginia: Time-Life Books, 1990), 70.

11. John Gribbin, *Timewarps* (New York: Delacorte Press/Eleanor Friede, 1979), 107.

12. By the Editors of Time-Life Books, *Time and Space: Mysteries of The Unknown* (Alexandria, Virginia: Time-Life Books, 1990), 75.

13. Ibid., 120.

14. Mark Nesbitt, *Ghosts of Gettysburg: Spirits, Apparitions and Haunted Places of the Battlefield* (Gettysburg, Pa., Thomas Publications, 1991), 58.

A Visitor From Another Century

1. Ammon Monroe Aurand, Jr., *The "Pow Wow" Book* (Harrisburg, Pa. By The Aurand Press., 1929). 5.

2. Ibid.

3. Ibid. 6

Last Room on the Left

1. Anne Fremantle and the Editors of Time-Life Books, *Age of Faith: Great Ages of Man, A History of the World's Cultures* (New York: Time Incorporated, 1965). 150.

2. Ibid. 162

3. Columbia Bicentennial Commission, *Columbia, Pennsylvania: Its People-Culture Religions Customs Education Vocations Industry.* 1977, 29.

4. John Ward Wilson Loose, Editor, *Journal of The Lancaster County Historical Society*, "Report of John Light Atlee, M.D.," Volume 61, 1957. 114.

5. John Ward Wilson Loose. 114.

An Unfair Trade

1. Roy Rivenburg, "Stoking The Fires Of Hell," *Lancaster Sunday News*, 16, January, 1994, A-9.

2. Ibid.

3. Ibid.

4. Ibid.

5. Ibid.

6. Ibid.

Beast in the Basement

1. J. I. Mombert, D.D., *An Authentic History Of Lancaster County In The State of Pennsylvania* (Lancaster, Pa.: J. E. Barr & Co., 1869), 610.

2. Columbia Bicentennial Commission, *Columbia, Pennsylvania: Its People-Culture Religions Customs Education Vocations Industry.* 1977., 3.

3. Mombert, 611.

4. Mombert, 612.

5. Mombert, 614.

6. H. W. Janson, *History of Art,* 3rd ed. revised and expanded by Anthony F. Janson (New York: Harry N. Abrams, Incorporated, 1986), 26, 27.

7. Ibid. 27

8. Ibid.

9. Ibid.

10. Ibid.

The Three Mile Isle of Misfortune

1. Elaine Huber, "A Nasty History During March, TMI Since 1904: Floods, Death, Destruction," *Lancaster Sunday News,* 23 March 1980, B1.

2. Dave Cody, "TMI: A History of Misfortune," *Lancaster Newspapers, Extra, North Central Edition,* 18 July 1984, 1.

3. Elaine Huber, "Three-Mile Island Had a Sometime Stormy Past," *The Lancaster Sunday News,* 4 July 1982, B3.

4. Ibid.

5. Ibid.

6. Ibid.

7. Ibid.

8. Ibid.

9. Ibid.

10. Elaine Huber, "Three Mile Island's Troubled History: 1762-1979," *Journal of the Lancaster County Historical Society*, Volume 91/1, 1987/1988. 3.

11. Ibid.

12. Ibid.

13. Ibid. 4.

14. Ibid.

15. Ibid. 5.

16. Ibid.

17. Huber, "A Nasty History During March, TMI Since 1904: Floods, Death, Destruction," B1.

18. Ibid. B3.

19. Ibid.

20. Huber, *Journal of The Lancaster County Historical Society*, 5.

21. Ibid.

22. Ibid.

23. Ibid.

24. Ibid.

25. Frank Muir, *An Irreverent and Thoroughly Incomplete Social History of Almost Anything* (New York: Stein and Day Publishers, 1976). 85.

Pennsylvania Pow Wow Doctors

1. Ammon Monroe Aurand, Jr., *The "Pow—Wow" Book* (Harrisburg, Pa.: Privately Printed By The Aurand Press, 1929), 20.

2. Ibid. 39.

3. Ibid. 43.

4. Ibid.

5. Ibid.

6. Ibid. 41.

7. Ibid. 55.

8. Ibid. 54.

9. Ibid. 42.

Who Are You Going to Call?

1. Robert R. Lyman, Sr., *Amazing Indeed, Strange Events In The Black Forest* (Coudersport, Pa.: Leader Publishing Company, 1973), 74.

2. Ibid.

Acknowledgements

*Whenever the literary German dives into a sentence, that is the last you are going to see of him till he emerges on the other side of his Atlantic with his verb in his mouth.

> Mark Twain
> A Connecticut Yankee At King Arthur's Court (1889) Ch. 22

About the Author

Dorothy Burtz Fiedel was born in Columbia, Pennsylvania. She graduated cum laude from Millersville University, Millersville, Pa. with a bachelor of science degree.

She is married and the mother of two sons and has two grandchildren.

A third book about ghosts and other mysteries is now being written by the author. This collection of true experiences will include stories from Pennsylvania and other states in the Union.

If you have had a strange experience and wish to share it, please write:

> Dorothy B. Fiedel
> 717 Kinderhook Road
> Columbia, Pa. 17512